ANIMAL SAFARI

Ostriches

by Kari Schuetz

BELLWETHER MEDIA · MINNEAPOLIS, MN

Note to Librarians, Teachers, and Parents:

Blastoff! Readers are carefully developed by literacy experts and combine standards-based content with developmentally appropriate text.

Level 1 provides the most support through repetition of high-frequency words, light text, predictable sentence patterns, and strong visual support.

Level 2 offers early readers a bit more challenge through varied simple sentences, increased text load, and less repetition of high-frequency words.

Level 3 advances early-fluent readers toward fluency through increased text and concept load, less reliance on visuals, longer sentences, and more literary language.

Level 4 builds reading stamina by providing more text per page, increased use of punctuation, greater variation in sentence patterns, and increasingly challenging vocabulary.

Level 5 encourages children to move from "learning to read" to "reading to learn" by providing even more text, varied writing styles, and less familiar topics.

Whichever book is right for your reader, Blastoff! Readers are the perfect books to build confidence and encourage a love of reading that will last a lifetime!

This edition first published in 2013 by Bellwether Media, Inc.

No part of this publication may be reproduced in whole or in part without written permission of the publisher. For information regarding permission, write to Bellwether Media, Inc., Attention: Permissions Department, 5357 Penn Avenue South, Minneapolis, MN 55419.

Library of Congress Cataloging-in-Publication Data
Schuetz, Kari.
  Ostriches / by Kari Schuetz.
    p. cm. – (Blastoff! readers: animal safari)
  Audience: 4-8.
  Audience: K to grade 3.
  Summary: "Developed by literacy experts for students in kindergarten through grade three, this book introduces ostriches to young readers through leveled text and related photos"– Provided by publisher.
  Includes bibliographical references and index.
  ISBN 978-1-60014-866-8 (hardcover : alk. paper)
  1. Ostriches–Juvenile literature. I. Title.
  QL696.S9S38 2013
  598.5'24–dc23   2012031233

Contents

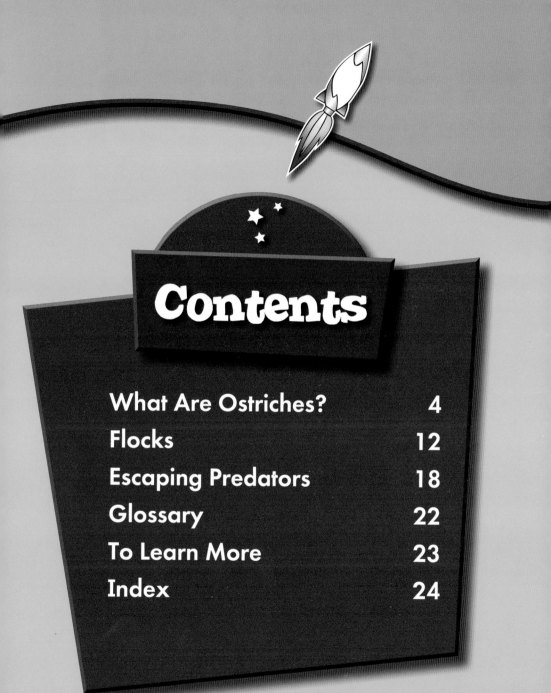

What Are Ostriches?

Ostriches are the largest birds on Earth.

They are too heavy to fly. They use their long legs to run fast.

Ostriches live in **savannahs** and deserts.

They eat seeds, leaves, and **roots**. Lizards and **insects** are also food.

Flocks

Ostriches travel in **flocks**. An **alpha pair** leads a flock.

Females in a flock lay eggs in one big nest. These are the largest of all bird eggs!

The alpha pair keeps the eggs warm until chicks **hatch**.

Escaping Predators

Ostriches sometimes lie in sand or soil to hide from **predators**.

Ostriches run from predators when they cannot hide. They are the fastest birds on land. Run, ostrich, run!

Glossary

alpha pair—the male and female in charge of an ostrich flock

flocks—groups of ostriches that live and travel together

hatch—to break out of an egg

insects—small animals with six legs and hard outer bodies; an insect's body is divided into three parts.

predators—animals that hunt other animals for food

roots—underground plants

savannahs—grasslands with scattered trees

To Learn More

AT THE LIBRARY

Kelly, Irene. *Even an Ostrich Needs a Nest: Where Birds Begin*. New York, N.Y.: Holiday House, 2009.

Lunis, Natalie. *Ostrich: The World's Biggest Bird*. New York, N.Y.: Bearport Pub., 2007.

Silverman, Buffy. *Can You Tell an Ostrich from an Emu?* Minneapolis, Minn.: Lerner Publications Company, 2012.

ON THE WEB

Learning more about ostriches is as easy as 1, 2, 3.

1. Go to www.factsurfer.com.

2. Enter "ostriches" into the search box.

3. Click the "Surf" button and you will see a list of related Web sites.

With factsurfer.com, finding more information is just a click away.

Index

The images in this book are reproduced through the courtesy of: Juan Martinez, front cover, p. 11 (right); J & C Sohns/Tier und Naturfotografie/SuperStock, p. 5; Jo Crebbin, p. 7; Nickolay Stanev, p. 9; Oleg Znamenskiy, p. 9 (left); Giancarlo Gagliardi, p. 9 (right); Gallo Images-Martin Harvey/Getty Images, p. 11; P. Uzunova, p. 11 (left); Travel Pictures Ltd/SuperStock, p. 13; Adrian Warren/Ardea/Animals Animals, p. 15; FLPA/Mike Powles/Age Fotostock, p. 17; Inga Spence/Getty Images, p. 19; National News/ZUMA Press/Newscom, p. 21.